Mindful SPACES

MINDFULNESS AND MY BODY

Written by Dr. Rhianna Watts and Katie Woolley

Illustrated by Sarah Jennings

For bulk sales to employers, member groups and health-related companies, contact Mayo Clinic at SpecialSalesMayoBooks@mayo.edu.

Proceeds from the sale of every book benefit important medical research and education at Mayo Clinic.

First American Edition 2024

MAYO CLINIC PRESS
200 First St. SW
Rochester, MN 55905
mcpress.mayoclinic.org

To stay informed about Mayo Clinic Press, please subscribe to our free e-newsletter at mcpress.mayoclinic.org or follow us on social media.

ISBN: 979-8-887-70131-8 (paperback) | 979-8-887-70132-5 (ebook) | 979-8-887-70117-2 (library binding)

Library of Congress Cataloging-in-Publication Data is available upon request.

MANUFACTURED IN CHINA

SAFETY PRECAUTIONS

We recommend adult supervision at all times while doing the exercises and activities in this book, particularly outdoors and activities involving exercise, glue, and scissors. When you are doing creative activities:

- Cover surfaces.
- Tie back long hair.
- Ask an adult for help with cutting.
- Check all ingredients for allergens.

Contents

WHAT IS MINDFULNESS?

Mindfulness is about becoming aware of what is going on inside your mind and body, as well as what is happening in the world around you. It is not about thinking about the past, or even what might happen in the future. Instead, it is about your body and your mind connecting with the world around you, right now.

Mindful exercises and activities can help you begin to focus on how your body feels and what you are thinking. Taking time to pause and understand yourself and what is happening around you, helps you get to know yourself and how you like to experience the world.

Make a Pinwheel

Ask a grown-up to help you make your very own pinwheel.

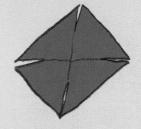

You will need: some color paper, scissors, glue, a split pin, and a pencil with an eraser.

1. Cut out one square, 2 inches by 2 inches.

2. Cut a line from each corner of your square, but not quite to the middle.

3. Place a blob of glue in the center of your square. Take the edge of fold 1 and stick the tip to the glue.

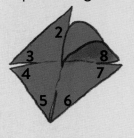

4. Then do tips 3, 5, and 7.

5. Push the split pin through the front to the back of your pin wheel and into the eraser on your pencil.

7. Then try and breathe normally.

6. Blow on your pinwheel using short, sharp breaths.

8. Which way of breathing works best?

HOW THIS ACTIVITY HELPS

This activity helps you see how your breath fills your body and how it affects what your body can do.

THE MIND AND THE BODY

Your body and your mind are busy places. They need to be healthy and active to do all the things you want to do, such as play with your friends, learn new things at school, and take part in activities and exercise.

Your body and your mind are tied together. If your thoughts and emotions become overwhelming, this can affect your body, and you may begin to feel stressed and anxious. You might feel butterflies in your tummy and your head might be full of worries.

Finding ways to calm your mind and your body, as well as become more aware of them, is a useful skill to have when life feels overwhelming.

Tense and Relax

Our bodies can often feel tight, coiled up as if ready to spring into action at any moment. Try this exercise to help you unwind.

1. Lie flat on the floor. How does your body feel on the ground?

2. Begin by letting your body relax into the ground beneath you, starting with your feet. When they are relaxed, notice what it feels like to tense and then relax them again.

3. Repeat step 2 with your leg muscles. Then your stomach and your back.

4. Finally repeat these steps with your shoulders and neck.

HOW THIS EXERCISE HELPS

This activity helps you learn to recognize signs of stress in your body, and what it feels like when you are relaxed. Relaxing your body can help calm your mind.

MINDFUL, NOT MIND FULL

Practicing mindfulness can calm your mind and help you concentrate on the present moment. Slowing down can give you time to choose how to respond to a situation.

It can also help you make sense of your busy thoughts and emotions so that you can feel better about yourself.

Body Scan

Imagine you are at the airport, about to go on vacation. First, you've got to go through the body scanner at the security desk.

What wouild the X-ray see in your body? What thoughts are in your head? What sensations are in your body and what emotions do you have?

HOW THIS EXERCISE HELPS

This activity helps you learn to notice what is happening with your mind, your body, and your emotions in the present moment, right here and right now.

9

MINDFUL BREATHS

One of the best mindful exercises to calm your body is to think about your breath. Your breath roots you in the present moment, helping you to focus on what is right in front of you. You can't forget about it or leave it behind. Your breath is always with you.

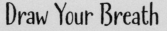

Activity

Draw Your Breath

Take a pen, pencil, or brush and some paper, and start to draw as you take a deep breath in. When you slowly release your breath, change the direction of the line. Repeat this action for a few moments. Then step back and look at your picture.

HOW THIS ACTIVITY HELPS

This activity helps you slow down and notice your breath, and what it feels like as you breathe air in and out of your body. Anytime you feel caught up, focus your attention on your breath for a few moments to slow down.

MINDFUL MOVEMENTS

Mindfulness is also about paying attention to the way your body moves and responds to the world around you. Your body feels different and behaves differently when you do different things.

How does your body feel when you are dancing? What is happening to your breath as you move? Are your breaths slow and deep, or quick and shallow? As you stretch and strengthen your muscles during exercise, do your arms and legs feel heavy or light?

What differences do you notice when you lie down and relax? How do you feel with the weight of your body pressing on the floor? How does the floor feel underneath you? Is it cool? Does it feel soft or is the surface hard?

Tiger Pose

Elephant Pose

Animal Yoga

All bodies are wonderful and they all move in different ways, just as animals move in different ways, too. Try these animal yoga poses!

Bear Cub Pose

Camel Pose

HOW THIS EXERCISE HELPS

This exercise helps you notice what your body feels like when you move in different ways. See if you can bring the same attention to everyday movements, like climbing in and out of bed!

MY SENSES

When you practice mindfulness and you begin to pause and pay more attention to the world, you become more curious. Your five senses can help you understand the world better.

Taste

Hear

See

Touch

Smell

For example, you use your sense of taste to choose and eat foods you enjoy. You use your sense of touch when you are planting seeds and push your hands into the cool, damp soil.

Five, Four, Three, Two, One

1. Notice five things that you can see. Try to spot things you wouldn't normally notice.
2. Notice four things you can feel. This brings your attention to textures and sensations on your skin.
3. Notice three things you can hear. Try to listen for sounds you often miss on a day-to-day basis.
4. Notice two things you can smell.
5. Notice one thing you can taste.

As you hunt for things using your senses, hold up your hand and trace around your fingers.

HOW THIS EXERCISE HELPS

Your senses connect you to the present—to what is happening to you right now. This can stop you from getting caught up in the past or the future.

SIGHT

Imagine looking at everything around you as if you are seeing it for the first time. What might you notice that you did not see before?

Looking at the world with a fresh perspective can help you find a new appreciation for things that have always been around you. Focusing your mind on one thing, like what you can see, can also help calm the racing thoughts in your head and relax your body.

Still Life Fruit

Think about a piece of fruit or other object you have at home and draw it from memory.

Then go and find this piece of fruit. Hold it in your hand in front you. Look at it as though you are seeing it for the first time. Notice its shape and its color. Feel its texture and its weight in your hand. Place the fruit in front of you, and look at it while you draw it.

Then compare your two drawings.

HOW THIS ACTIVITY HELPS

This activity teaches you to look at your world with curiosity, as if you have not seen it before, to help you spot new sights that you may have missed in the past. See if you can bring this new way of seeing into daily life, like on your journey to and from school!

SOUND

Take a moment to pause and just listen. Start to notice that sounds behave in a similar way to the sensations in your body and the thoughts in your mind. A sound comes and goes, and, as each one disappears, it doesn't leave a trace. There can even be silence until a new sound appears.

If your mind starts to wander, don't worry. Bring your attention back to your hearing and see what new sound you can tune into.

Ring the Bell!

The sound of a bell can help you refocus your attention, allowing you to concentrate on one task.

1. Lie down on the floor and close your eyes.
2. Ask someone else to ring a bell.
3. Listen to the sound it makes until it disappears.
4. Raise your hand when the sound stops.

HOW THIS EXERCISE HELPS

This exercise helps you learn to notice sounds around you, and how they come and go, just like our experiences come and go, too.

SMELL

Your sense of smell is your most powerful sense. The smell of baking cookies can bring comfort. The smell of smoke can warn you of danger. The smell of food can remind you that you are hungry. You need your sense of smell to be able to taste, too!

When you use your sense of smell in a mindful way, you are paying more attention to what you can smell, how that smell makes you feel, and how it affects your thoughts.

Next time you have clean bedsheets, take a moment to bury your head in the fabric. Spend a few moments smelling its fresh scent. What do you notice in your nostrils? How does this smell make you feel in your body and in your mind?

Lavender Modeling Clay

You use your sense of smell every day, and it is a wonderful tool when you are playing, too. Try making this lavender modeling clay. Then use it to create shapes and patterns.

You will need: An adult to help, 1 cup of plain flour, 1 cup of salt, 4 cups of water, ½ cup cream of tartar, 10 tablespoons of vegetable oil, and 2-3 drops of lavender oil.

1. With an adult, mix the flour, salt, water, cream of tartar, and oil in a saucepan.

2. Ask an adult to heat the mixture until it forms a dough. Allow it to cool in the pan.

4. You can store your modeling clay in an airtight container for about four weeks.

HOW THIS ACTIVITY HELPS

Lavender aids sleep and helps you feel less restless. Playing with the dough with your hands as you smell the lavender helps you focus on the activity without your mind wandering.

3. Ask an adult to add the lavender oil to the dough. Knead it for a minute or two.

TASTE

It is human nature to eat quickly when we are hungry!
When life is busy and you are doing homework, reading a book,
or playing a computer game, you may not really notice what
you are eating. Taking the time to slow down and enjoy
your food takes practice!

Being mindful of the food you eat means noticing
where it comes from and how it is grown or produced.
It means learning about how it is harvested and cooked,
and how it tastes.

Mindful Eating

1. Try and eat your dinner when you feel a little bit hungry but not yet starving. This will give you time to enjoy your food, rather than rush to fill your stomach!
2. Use all your senses! Notice the colors of the food, the textures, and the smells.
3. Chew your food slowly, thinking about how the ingredients taste and any flavors you might recognize.
4. Be grateful for the food you are enjoying.

HOW THIS EXERCISE HELPS

How you eat goes a long way to helping you live a happy, healthy life. Slowing down and using your sense of taste to mindfully eat helps you understand where your food comes from, so you can appreciate it all the more. It will also help you know when you are full and ready to stop eating.

TOUCH

One of the best ways to become more mindful is to develop an awareness of touch. We feel things constantly, every single day, but because we use our sense of touch so often, it is common for us to ignore it.

Tuning into your sense of touch helps keep you calm, as you find ways to rest your body. You can use your sense of touch to soothe yourself when you are upset, for example, by having a relaxing bubble bath or by cuddling your pet. You can also calm your body when you feel anxious by paying attention to the feel of your feet when they are firmly on the ground.

Balloon Stress Ball

This stress ball is easy to make and calming to use!
You will need: An adult to help, a balloon, some flour, and a plastic bottle.

1. Ask an adult to help you fill your bottle with flour. Watch out, it can be messy!

2. Stretch your balloon and put it over the open end of your bottle.

3. Tip the flour into the balloon until it is about half full.

4. Carefully remove the balloon from the bottle.

5. Let out as much air as possible, then tie a knot.

HOW THIS ACTIVITY HELPS

Touching and manipulating an object can help focus your mind when you feel restless.

SENSE THE START OF THE DAY

How you start your morning can set you up for how the rest of your day unfolds. Being mindful of your body, your senses, and your thoughts, and emotions during your daily routine can help you focus on the present moment.

7 am: Wake up and get dressed.
How does your body feel as you stretch? Do you feel relaxed after a good night's sleep? How do your clothes feel against your skin?

7:30 am: Eat your breakfast.
Where did your breakfast come from? Is it hot or cold? How does it feel as you chew? What flavors can you taste?

8 am: Brush your teeth.
How do your teeth feel when you brush them? What movements are you doing as you brush your teeth?

8:30 am: Go to school.
What do you notice all around you?
What sounds can you hear? What things
can you see? What can you touch?

If you are riding a bike, use the pedals as an anchor for your thoughts. Focus on the repetitive movements of your feet on the pedals to help stop your mind from wandering.

As you go through your day, try and include other mindful moments in your routine to help your mind stay focused and your body calm and content.

Activity

Mindful Check-in

When you wake in the morning, write down how your body feels. What emotions are present? Is your mind calm or already racing ahead to school? Note how your body feels—is it comfortable or tense? It might help to draw how your body feels, too.

HOW THIS ACTIVITY HELPS

Becoming more mindful and aware of what is happening in your mind, and with your emotions and your body, takes practice. Starting every morning with a mindful moment can help you begin the day as you mean to go on!

SHOULD I GO?

Mindfulness gives you tools to reduce any stress and worry that could come and go at any moment. Being able to slow down and notice how your body feels and thinks gives you time to understand yourself better, so that you know how you want to respond before you actually do!

Red – Stop. Take some deep breaths in and out.

Yellow – Wait and watch. What is happening around you? What is happening inside your body and your mind?

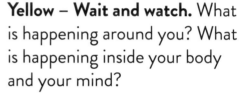

Green – Go! But go carefully and mindfully. This could be continuing to do the activity you are doing or finding something else that brings you calm.

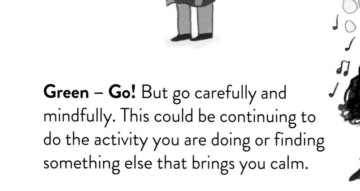

One calming activity is creating and crafting objects. Making crafts practices the skills of focus and concentration. It is relaxing and gives you time to think about your emotions. You can choose how to express yourself with the crafts you make and the decorations you choose, helping you trust your ideas and yourself!

Traffic Light Paper Chains

You will need: red, yellow, and green paper, scissors, glue.

1. Ask an adult to help you cut out strips of paper using your scissors.
2. Take one green strip and glue the ends to form a circle.
3. Thread an yellow strip through the circle and glue the ends together.
4. Repeat step 3 with a red strip.
5. Keep alternating between the colors until you've got a long paper chain.
6. You could hang you chain across your bedroom window, to remind you of your mindfulness practice when you wake up every morning!

HOW THIS ACTIVITY HELPS

When you are learning a new skill, it can be helpful to use visual reminders. Traffic lights remind drivers to stop and wait before driving off. Your paper chain can help you remember to slow down and respond to situations more mindfully, too.

MINDFULNESS TIPS

Mindfulness helps anchor you in the present moment.
It helps you feel confident and ready to tackle the day,
and it can help you navigate big emotions, while allowing you
to find moments of calm in your busy world.

Here are some tips to help you practice mindfulness.

* You can practice mindfulness anywhere and at any time. Mindfulness simply means choosing to pay attention to what is happening inside your mind and body, and what is happening around you, in the present moment, right here and right now.

* You can do this by sitting and focusing on your breath for five minutes in bed before you go to sleep, or you could do this by focusing on what you can see and hear while walking to school.

* Your breath and how it feels in your body is very important. Paying attention to your breath helps you focus on what is happening in the present moment. Your breath is like an anchor for your mind and body. It can stop them from floating away.

* It's okay if you start to feel a little bored or your mind wanders. If you can, just notice this and refocus your mind where you want it to be. If you get stuck, be kind to yourself. Remember you are learning a new skill and you can always try again another day.

* If your body starts to feel uncomfortable, notice where in your body you feel any aches and move so you are in a more comfortable position. However, always stop doing an exercise if you feel pain.

INDEX